BACKYARD BIRDS OF Florida